Trains

WHITE STAR PUBLISHERS

CONTENTS

1
With high-speed travel, the railways entered
the third millennium.

2-3
An ultramodern Chinese Railways high speed
CRH2 series train.

Text
FRANCO TANEL

Graphic design
PAOLA PIACCO

INTRODUCTION

In the middle of the 19th century, the invention of the steam engine and the building of the first railways were a true revolution. The world became smaller and for the first time in history people and goods could be transported quickly. Within a few decades, the train, the child and at the same time progenitor of the Industrial Revolution, had spread around the world. Even by the early years of the 20th century, locomotives were exceeding the then astonishing speed of 60 miles per hour (100km/h) and passenger cars were comfortable vehicles in which to travel the length and breadth of Europe. The first international trains were born, such as the legendary Imperial Indian Mail train which linked London to the port of Brindisi.

4
The huge Milwaukee Road EP-2 "Bipolar" from 1925.

5
The historic American locomotive Jupiter at the Golden Spike National Historic Site.

But even as steam locomotive design was evolving towards more powerful and faster models, electricity was already being applied to railway traction. The electric locomotives were more powerful and less complex to manage. In the 1930s the first heat engines appeared: initially light vehicles for passenger transport, which then became heavier and more powerful locomotives. Technological progress, however, was not sufficient in the '60s to deal with the competition from road transport, which was more flexible and eco-nomical; a profound crisis from which the train emerged at the end of the '80s thanks to new high speed trains for passenger transport and intermodality in freight. An awareness of environmental issues has brought the dear old train back to center stage, a means of transport which is now comfortable and tech-nological but also environmentally friendly.

6-7
A Shinkansen races in front of Mount Fuji: two symbols of Japan.

8-9
The wonderful Swiss tourist train the Bernina Express beside Lago Bianco.

Chapter 1

STEAM LOCOMOTIVES

As happens with most discoveries, the train too is the fruit of the insights and often obscure work of many men, which developed over time until the moment when all these efforts were sublimated in an invention that changed the world.

Since ancient times it had been known that the wheel performs better if it can run along a smooth, flat surface. The ancient Romans paved their main roads with a double row of stones as far apart as the wheels of animal-drawn carts. It is curious to note that the distance between the grooves left on these stones by the repeated passage of cartwheels, measured in the archaeological excavations at Pompeii, is only two-tenths of an inch (half a centimeter) narrower than the standard gauge of railways (56-and-a-half inches or 1,435 mm), i.e., the distance between the internal faces of the two rails.

10
The English locomotive Wylam Dilly in a photo from 1862: it has survived to the present day.

Fig. 58.—Working Coal in the thick coal of South Staf

Documents dating back to the 12th century show how, in the mines of Alsace, coal was transported by horse-drawn carts with flanged wheels that ran on wooden rails. A system which, employed with many variables, quickly spread to most of the mines in Europe. Around the mid-1700s, with the development of metalworking, it was natural to replace the wood, which wore out quickly, with bars of cast iron first and then iron. They were kept the right distance apart by wooden sleepers: to all intents and purposes this was already a primordial track and it was probably because they adapted the wagons then in use that the measure of the normal distance between the two rails was precisely that between the wheels of these vehicles, four feet eight-and-a-half inches (1,435 mm). At the beginning of the 19th century in Great Britain in the mines and ports long lines of wagons loaded with coal were pulled by horses, but everything would have stopped here if a way had not been found to replace animal traction.

12-13
Wagons on rails pulled by horses in South Staffordshire in an engraving from the time.

14
James Watt's first project for a steam locomobile, an ancestor of the locomotive.

15
The steam engine invented in 1772 by Newcomen to pump water from mines.

In the early 18th century, Thomas Newcomen, taking up the studies of the Frenchman Papin, built the first proper steam engine, managing to convert the energy contained in the steam itself into mechanical movement. This rudimentary machine immediately found a use in the mines emptying tunnels of stagnant water. In 1765, James Watt, having restored one, after four years of work built a much more efficient and economic model that spread rapidly in many factories throughout Great Britain, contributing in a fundamental way to the start of what would later be called the "Industrial Revolution."

NEWCOMEN'S, *Atmospheric STEAM ENGINE for draining Mines,*

constructed by Mr. Smeaton 1772.

PLATE II.

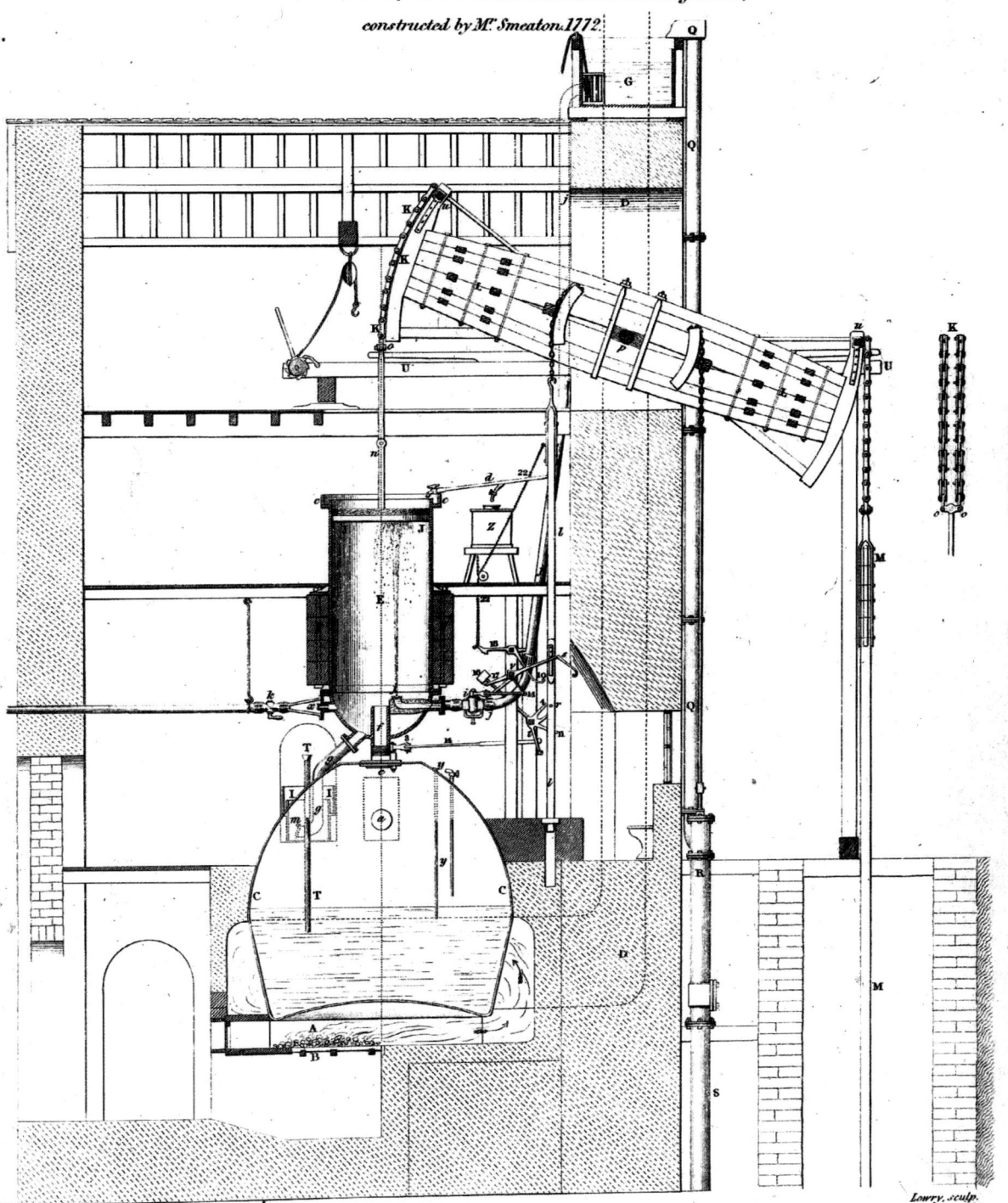

Farey, delin.

Lowry, sculp.

0 1 2 3 4 5 6 7 8 9 10 11 12 13 14 15 16 17 18 19 20 21 22 23 24 25 26 27 28 29 30 31 32 feet

But the steam engine was still immobile: the turning point came with its use on a vehicle. The first person to build a primitive locomotive was Richard Trevithick who, in 1804, put into service a rudimentary vehicle on the Pennydarren Tramroad in Wales. The machine, which pulled convoys of 27.1 tons (25 metric tons), was equipped with a single large cylinder and a huge flywheel acting through a series of gears on the left-hand wheels. The driver was not on board but drove the vehicle walking alongside it. To publicize his invention in 1808 in London Trevithick organized a circular circuit where a new model of locomotive drove at speeds of up to 12.4 mph (20 km/h) pulling a carriage adapted for rails. The machine was called "Catch me who can" and for a shilling people could have a ride on the train. Unfortunately, a broken rail and the resulting derailment brought the spectacle to an end.

16-17
The exhibition of Richard Trevithick's locomotive at Euston Square in 1809.

d Trevithick's Railroad Euston Square 1809

18
A period image of the Locomotion,
the first steam locomotive built
by George Stephenson.

18-19
The "Puffing Billy" locomotive built between
1813 and 1814 by William Hedley.

In the years that followed other inventors successfully built working locomotives: Matthew Murray and John Blenkinsop for Middleton Colliery Railway, while William Hedley and Christopher Blackett built the locomotive that history knows as Puffing Billy for the Wylam Colliery Railway.

George Stephenson, recognized by all as the inventor of the steam locomotive, also worked on a locomotive, known as Blucher for Killingworth Mine. In the years following 1814, Stephenson built other locomotives until Edward Pease, a mining entrepreneur from Darlington got permission to build a 24-mile (39 km) railway to the docks at Stockton-on-Tees. On 25 September 1825 the first train, led for

safety by a man on horseback, and pulled by a small locomotive called "Locomotion" traveled its full length, effectively launching the new age of rail transport. Five years later the Liverpool – Manchester line was opened to traffic, which can be considered the first real commercial rail line in the world for passengers and goods.

20
The British Rail Class 2P and Royal Scot, 1956.

20-21
A final polish for the LNER, 1933.

Chapter 2

ELECTRIC AND DIESEL TRACTION

THE ONLY EXPERIENCE OF USING ELECTRICITY IN TRANSPORT ON RAIL UP THE TO THE END OF THE 19TH CENTURY WAS THE TRAM. IN 1879, THE ENGINEER WERNER VON SIEMENS HAD PRESENTED AT THE BERLIN TRADE FAIR A SORT OF SMALL ELECTRIC VEHICLE, POWERED THROUGH A CENTRAL RAIL WHICH RAN ON A NARROW-GAUGE TRACK. IT WAS LITTLE MORE THAN A FAIRGROUND ATTRACTION, BUT IT COULD PULL ABOUT 30 PEOPLE ALONG A TRACK OF 886 FEET (270 METERS). IT WAS THE FIRST EXAMPLE OF THE APPLICATION OF ELECTRICAL POWER TO A RAIL VEHICLE. TWO YEARS LATER, IN GREAT BRITAIN, A SHORT 2 FEET (610 MM) GAUGE LINE WAS INAUGURATED, POWERED BY 110V FROM A THIRD RAIL, THROUGH THE FOREST OF BRIGHTON, WHICH IS CONSIDERED TO HAVE BEEN THE FIRST ELECTRIC RAILWAY IN THE WORLD.

22
The first electric locomotive built by Werner von Siemens
for the Berlin Fair of 1879.

The first important application was in 1895, when, in the United States, Baltimore & Ohio built three direct-current electric locomotives to replace the steam locomotives in the city tunnel of about one-and-a-quarter miles (2 kilometers) of Howard Street in Baltimore. The potential of electric traction was confirmed in 1901

in Germany where two electric locomotives built by technicians from Siemens and AEG, supplied an alternating three-phase current at 10,000 volts and 50 Hz through an overhead line, reached 99.4 mph (160 km/h), and then 128 mph (206 km/h) on the 14.3 miles (23 km) of the line between Marienfelde and Zossen.

24-25
The electric locomotive that B&O used from 1895 for service in the Howard Street Tunnel.

25
The Baltimore & Ohio Railroad electric current generators from around 1895.

SWITZERLAND
S^T GOTHARD LINE

26
A poster from 1924 celebrating the completion
of the famous Gothard Alpine railway.

27
The speed of the new German steam seen
in an illustration from 1926.

The Italian State Railways were among the first in the world to take concrete action to develop an electric drive system suitable for towing heavy trains over long distances, adopting the three-phase current at 3,000 V on the Valtellina lines as early as 1902. Germany, Switzerland and Austria instead chose to wait for a technological evolution that allowed the use of single-phase alternating current of 15,000 V. The three-phase power supply adopted in Italy in fact required a double contact wire which created major complications on the exchanges and, because of the frequencies adopted, limited trains to fixed speeds. In 1928, therefore, the Italian State Railways (FS) decided to adopt 3,000 V DC (for a single contact wire) for subsequent electrifications, which became the national standard. France instead first used electrification at 1,500 V DC and subsequently at 25,000 V AC. These differences reflect the birth of the railway networks in Europe, which were conceived as separate national systems for both political and military reasons.

Also for this reason, each national rail network developed its own locomotives. We will briefly look at some of the locomotives that have made the history of the electric railway. We start with an FS locomotive, the E550, built in 1908: with five coupled axes, it was supplied by 3,600 V three-phase AC at 16 2/3 Hz, designed for pulling heavy trains on the difficult Giovi line between the port of Genoa and Turin. On these slopes two coupled locomotives hauled freight trains of 418 tons (380 metric tons) at 31 mph (50 km/h), while the steam locomotives could only manage 143 tons (130 metric tons) at 15.5 mph (25 km/h). When the FS chose direct current in 1928, they built another symbolic locomotive, the E626 of which 448 were made, many of which remained in service until the end of the 1990s.

28-29
The E626 electric locomotives of the Italian
Railways came into service in 1927.

30-31
The Pennsylvania Railroad GG1 electric
locomotive in Broad Street Station in
Philadelphia.

31
An illustration from the '40s celebrates
the streamlined locomotives of the
Pennsylvania Railroad.

In the mid-'30s in the United States, the Pennsylvania Railroad built 139 examples of the GG1, a powerful single-phase AC locomotive intended for the principal passenger trains on the network. With an output of 3,660 kW it pulled at 100 mph (160 km/h) trains of 20 carriages and weighing 1,763 tons (1,600 metric tons).

Just as well-known was the French CC7107: only one was built but it became famous for beating the world speed record with 206 mph (331 km/h) in 1955. Mention must also be made of the 139 and 140 of the DB, the true backbone of the German set-up from the mid-'50s onwards. About 900 were built in total, intended for the towing of both passenger and goods trains. In 1964, the SNCF built the CC 40100, the first multivoltage locomotives, capable of moving under four different types of power supply. Ahead of their time, they only traveled between France and Belgium, but highlighted the need to aim for interoperability on the network in Europe, a goal that is being reached, in part, only today.

32-33
The French Railways BB 9004 established the world speed in 1955 with a record 206 mph (331 km/h).

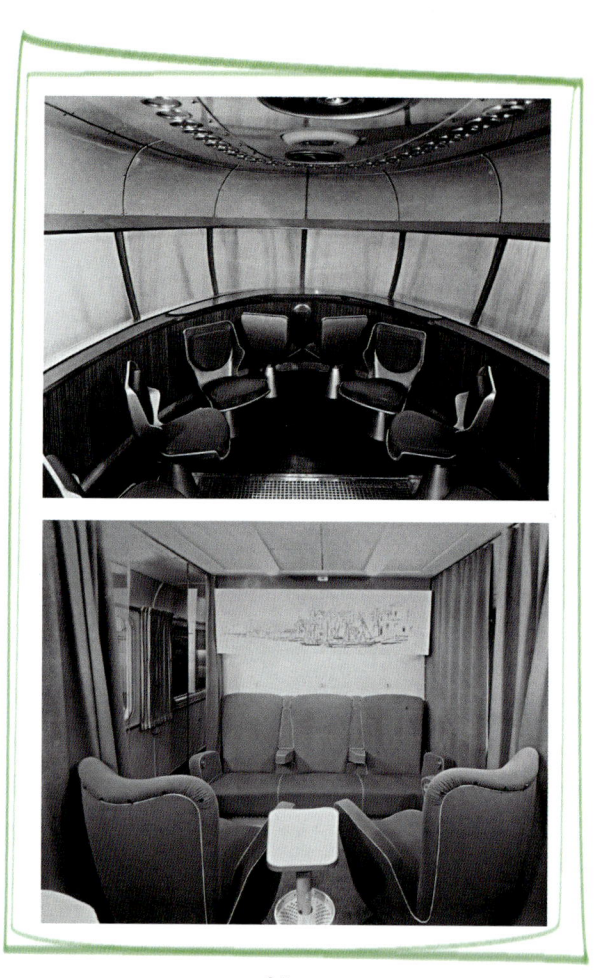

34 top
The observation lounge of the Settebello electric
train with swivel seats.

34 bottom
One of the lounge compartments of the ETR 300.

34-35
The famous luxury ETR 300 Settebello electric
train of the Italian Railways in 1952.

The Burlington Road Zephyr train was so light it could be moved by hand (1934).

The first important applications were in the '30s, in the U.S., when they were adopted as generators for the electric motors of self-propelling trains such as the Burlington Zephyr. On much smaller and lighter vehicles such as railcars, diesel engines were also used with mechanical transmission, as on the Italian diesel rail cars, the Aln 56 and Aln 556 by Breda and Fiat. The question became more complex when dealing with heavy train locomotives. In this case, from the end of the '30s, the United States followed the path of electrical transmission while Germany focused on hydraulic transmission. The greater development in diesel traction was thanks to the American railroads, also due to their choice not to electrify, for cost reasons, lines which were often thousands of kilometers long, except in urban areas.

38-39
The F7 diesel locomotive built by General Motors Kansas City Southern Railroad.

39
Presentation of the Paris-Brussels electric traction link on September 9, 1963.

General Motors (GM), with its Electro-Motive Division, was a protagonist with legendary locomotives such as the F-Series of which over 7,000 were built from 1939 onwards and the GP Series, which stands for "general purpose," of which 10,647 were built from 1949. More recent but equally

important are the DD40 AX built for Union Pacific and the SD 40-2 of which more than 4,000 models have been sold. In Europe it is worth recalling the Deltic BR 55 and BR 47 of British Rail, the BB 67000 of the French Railways (all diesel-electric), and the V200 of the DB (diesel-hydraulic).

Chapter 3

HIGH SPEED

THE HISTORY OF HIGH SPEED RAIL TRAVEL GOES BACK A LONG WAY: RAILWAY AUTHORITIES HAD ALWAYS SOUGHT TO IMPROVE THE PERFORMANCE OF THEIR TRAINS. IN 1938, THE BRITISH A4 MALLARD LOCOMOTIVE SET THE SPEED RECORD FOR STEAM ENGINES WITH 125 MPH (202 KM/H), AND THE GERMAN SERIES 05 LOCOMOTIVES, OF THE DR, REACHED SPEEDS OF UP TO 126 MPH (203 KM/H). TODAY, THOUGH, WHAT IS MEANT BY HIGH SPEED TRAINS ARE SPECIALLY DESIGNED TRAINS TRAVELING ON DEDICATED LINES AT SPEEDS ABOVE 155 MPH (250 KM/H). THE DEVELOPMENT AND SPREAD OF HIGH SPEED LINES HAS HELPED TO CREATE A SORT OF COMEBACK OF THE TRAIN WITH RESPECT TO AIR AND ROAD ON DISTANCES BETWEEN 200 AND 400 MILES (300 AND 600 KM). THE HIGH SPEED TRAIN PROVIDES DIRECT ACCESS TO CITY CENTERS WITHOUT THE WAITING AND TRANSFER TIMES AT AIRPORTS, IT IS MUCH FASTER THAN THE CAR AND ALLOWS PASSENGERS TO WORK, CONVENIENTLY CONNECTED TO THE INTERNET.

40
The famous British A4 "Mallard" locomotive,
which set the speed record of 126 mph (203 km/h).

The high speed train as a system of specialized vehicles and infrastructure was born in the mid-'60s in Japan and its symbol is the train we know as Shinkansen. In fact, for the Japanese "Shinkansen" simply means "new railway" and refers to the first line between Tokaido and Osaka which opened in 1964. The trains are identified by a serial number depending on the model and have nicknames. So the first train was Series 0 "Kodama," i.e., Thunder, a train that was revolutionary at the time: 16 cars, all motorized, about a quarter of a mile (400 meters) long, powered by 25kV AC and capable of a top speed of 130 mph (210 km/h). Over the decades, the Japanese network has expanded and developed with speeds today of 200 mph (320 km/h) and there are now numerous series of trains in service on the network. Since then, high speed trains around the world, while adopting different technological solutions, have shared a similar concept: aerodynamic design, a fixed two-way composition with the possibility of joining trains together.

42-43
A modern Japanese high speed train
dashes in front of Mount Fuji.

A front view of the Italo high speed train, belonging to the Italian private company NTV.

As regards the electrical power supply, the most widespread is 25kV AC which allows easier management of the great power involved, while transmission can be distributed or concentrated. In the case of distributed transmission, all or almost all the elements of the train sit on engine trucks, while in concentrated transmission the train has two engines at either end which enclose a variable number of towed carriages. The "Pendolino" ETR 600 and ETR 610 of the Italian Railways and the Italo NTV (Nuovo Trasporto Viaggiatori - New Passenger Transport) have distributed transmission; the TGV of the French Railways, the Frecciarossa ETR 500 of the Italian Railways but also the first ICE of the German Railways employ concentrated transmission. High speed is a system, not just a train, and so we must also mention the specialized infrastructure. To be able to travel at speeds of over 186 mph (300 km/h), the lines are designed with very broad curves, a greater distance between the tracks than on traditional lines, and special safety and traffic-control systems. Here too different philosophies of construction have developed: the French provide lines dedicated exclusively to high speed trains, while the Italians and Germans instead design lines that can also be traveled on by freight or other "traditional" trains. The main difference is that the track gradient in the French case can reach 35 per thousand while on the Italian lines it does not normally exceed 18 per thousand. It seems a tiny difference, but in reality it translates into extra bridges, viaducts and tunnels to be built to keep the track as "flat" as possible. In terms of technologies for safety and speed control, Italy leads the world, having adopted the ERTMS (European Rail Traffic Management System) Level 2 system on all 620 miles (1,000 km) of its high speed network. This is an advanced management, control and protection system for rail traffic and related signaling, designed to replace the multiple and mutually incompatible movement and safety systems of the various European railways with a view to ensuring the interoperability of trains especially on the new high speed networks on the Continent.

Born in Japan and developed in Europe, high speed rail has now spread around the world. We look at some of the main trains starting with the French TGV. Designed by Alstom, it was launched in 1978 with the TGV PSE version, and was then made in numerous other versions, the most recent of which is the TGV 2N2, or Duplex Nouvelle Generation, on two levels. TGV connections also extend to Belgium, Holland and

Germany. We should remember that on April 3, 2007 on the Paris-Strasbourg line, a specially equipped TGV set the world speed record for rail reaching 357.2 mph (574.8 km/h).

46-47
A French TGV at full speed: the transalpine network extends throughout the country.

In Germany the high speed trains are known as ICE (Inter City Express): since 1991, when the first generation, ICE 1, entered service to date, another series has been developed with very different features: ICE 2, with a single engine at one end and a driver's cab at the other; ICE 3 with distributed rather than concentrated power as in the earlier versions; and finally ICE T and ICE TD with a tilting body thanks to the technology of the Alstom Pendolino, also in a diesel version. In reality, these last two trains are intended for non-high speed lines where thanks to the tilting they respectively reach 143 and 124 mph (230 and 200 km/h). The FyraV250 trains, instead, built by the Italian company Ansaldo Breda, recently entered service between Belgium and the Netherlands.

48-49
A German Railways ICE 3 high speed train on the Frankfurt-Cologne line.

The scenario in Italy varies widely with Trenitalia, the railway company of the Gruppo FS Italiane relying on the FS ETR 500 known as the Frecciarossa (186 mph / 300 km/h top speed) for connections on the Turin-Milan-Rome-Naples-Salerno route and the ETR 600 and 610 Frecciargento, while the private operator NTV (Nuovo Trasporto Viaggiatori) relies on the Alstom AGV electric trains known as Italo.

50
NTV's high speed Italo train was built by the French company Alstom.

50-51
Two Italian Railways ETR 500 trains beneath the vaults of the Central Station in Milan.

CRH380A-6095L

Among the latest and most modern Japanese high speed trains we recall the E6 Series of JR East and the N700 of JR West. In China, the second generation of high speed trains is designed to reach 336 mph (380 km/h) in commercial service: there are four series of trains classified as CHR380A made entirely

by the Chinese manufacturer CSL&RSC Ltd, CHR380B and C developed in a joint venture with Siemens, and the CHR380D made in partnership with Bombardier. Two families of trains instead operate on the South Korean high speed network: the KTX-I derived from the French TGV and the KTX-II manufactured by Hyundai Rotem.

52-53
A Chinese high speed train, CRH 380A, stopped at Wuhan Station.

53
A trial run for the Japanese high speed train Komachi E6 in Sendai Station.

As was the case with electric loco-motives, today the great rolling-stock manufacturers have developed modular platforms for high speed trains from which the trains built for the various railway companies are derived. The main platforms are the TGV, Pendolino and AGV of Alstom, Bombardier Zefiro, (from which the ETR 1000 is also derived), the Siemens Velaro (ICE 3 in Germany, but also the Sapsan for the Russian Railways, and the AVE103 for Spain) and the Talgo by the manufacturer of the same name.

54 top
Two Talgo 350 high speed trains of the Spanish Railways in Valencia.

54 bottom
The repair workshops of the Russian Sapsan
train which links Moscow to Saint Petersburg.

54-55
A French Thalys high speed train stopped at
the German station of Cologne.

Chapter 4

TOURIST TRAINS

56
The luxurious interiors of the tourist train the Orient Express which offers
numerous itineraries across Europe.

Railway and tourism are really a perfect combination: in every corner of the world it is possible to find a train or a railway line that might inspire a journey. Of course, some are luxury trains, but we will see that it is not necessary to lay out substantial sums, because it really is possible to find something to suit every budget. Naturally, the imagination turns immediately to the "prince" of trains, the legendary Orient Express. This train, which from 1883 linked the Paris Gare de l'Est station to Istanbul, no longer exists, but since 1982 its charms have been revived by the Venice Simplon Orient Express. The train, made up of beautifully restored vintage carriages, regularly travels along various European routes including London - Paris - Venice, Paris - Bucharest - Budapest - Istanbul, but also Venice - Krakow - Dresden - London. A journey of absolute luxury in a 1920s atmosphere is a present worth indulging in at least once in a lifetime.

58-59
The Orient Express between London and Dover, unusually being pulled by a steam locomotive.

60
The journey in the bar of the tourist train the Orient Express is also accompanied by piano.

60-61
Passengers on the Royal Scotsman luxury train are welcomed by the sound of bagpipes.

Equally prestigious is the Royal Scotsman whose passengers are greeted by pipers in traditional dress. The train sets out from Edinburgh and offers a variety of routes in the north of Scotland.

62
The very luxurious breakfast served aboard
the Al Andalus Express.

62-63
The Al Andalus Express luxury train at
Seville Station in Spain.

For those who prefer the sun of southern Europe, Spain offers two beautiful luxury trains, the Transcantabrico and El Al Andalus. The first runs on narrow-gauge tracks in northern Spain: the tourist route connects San Sebastian and Santiago de Compostela but the journey by train runs between Bilbao and Ferrol. The second travels on the broad-gauge Spanish rail network and proposes two classic routes: Madrid - Saragossa and the circular route starting and finishing in Seville. Both these trains offer perfectly restored vintage carriages to provide the atmosphere of the great luxury trains of the early 1900s.

64-65
A photo taken from the window of a train on the Trans-Siberian near Irkutsk.

65
The crew of the Indian luxury train the Palace on Wheels posing in Udaipur Station.

We cannot overlook two great luxury trains in Russia: launched in 2007, the Golden Eagle Trans-Siberian Express repeats the success of the Grand Trans-Siberian Express which had already been operating for some years. The first offers its passengers the backdrop of the Silk Road and Mongolia, the second the classic route of the Trans-Siberian Railway from Moscow to Vladivostok. In India it is worth tak-

ing a trip on the Palace on Wheels which provides a taste of the Maharaja: it is a veritable palace on rails whose carriages are decorated with tapestries, carvings and silks that tell the history of the country. Renovated in 2009, it passes through Rajasthan with an 8-day tour that takes in the main towns of the state.

66-67
The Australian tourist train the Ghan leaves
Alice Spings: in the background the outline
of the MacDonnell Ranges.

67
The South African tourist train Pride
of Africa leaves Pretoria pulled by
a steam locomotive.

Moving to Australia, the Ghan is the dream train, one that in 48 hours crosses the continent from north to south, linking Darwin to Adelaide. It is a journey of 1,851 miles (2,979 km), which also passes through the city of Alice Springs and retraces the route of the camel caravans which were known here as "The Afghan Express" (from which the train takes its name), crossing the desert

heart of Australia. In Africa we find the Blue Train from Pretoria to Cape Town, but also on the same route The Pride of Africa, often pulled by a period steam locomotive.

68-69
The Rocky Mountains provide the backdrop
for a Canadian Pacific goods train.

69
The PeruRail train climbs through the forest
to reach the archeological site of Machu
Picchu.

But to enjoy a thrilling train journey it is also possible to choose much cheaper solutions. In Germany, for example, it is possible to experience the charm of a small railway network which is further animated by steam locomotives: we are talking about the Harz Railway which has as its center Nordhausen, a town along the Kassel-Halle main line. In this paradise for lovers of historical trains the uphill stretch from Wernigerode to Brocken is covered only by steam trains. In Switzerland at least one trip on the trains of the Rhaetian Railway is a must. In this case the trains perform both a regular public transport service

and one for tourists: the Bernina Express and Glacier Express trains are unforgettable. In July 2008, the stretch between Thusis and Tirano of the Rhaetian Railway was named by UNESCO as a World Heritage Site.

Between Switzerland and Austria, also worth visiting is the Vigezzina railway which connects Domodossola to Locarno. In Austria it is possible to visit the Zillertalbahn, a small narrow-gauge railway (30 inches/760 mm), which goes from Jenbach to Mayrhofen. At Jenbach another small railway begins, the Achenseebahn, narrow-

gauge as well (but 39.4 inches/1,000 mm) with steam and a rack portion. Jenbach is the only railway location in Austria where there are three distinct railway gauges and it is easy to reach, situated as it is on the main line from Innsbruck to Salzburg.

70
The Bernina Express, one of the most famous Alpine tourist trains near the Bernina Pass.

70-71
A splendid winter view of the Harz tourist train in Germany.

In Great Britain there are dozens and dozens of tourist lines. We will mention just two in particular. The Bluebell Railway, the first British standard-gauge rail line preserved and managed entirely by volunteers since 1960, which only uses steam trains and is one of the major tourist attractions

in Sussex; and the Talyllin Central Railway in Wales which still uses original period locomotives and carriages.

72-73
A short train on the small tourist Bluebell Railway in West Sussex.

73
A view of a small station on the tourist Bluebell Railway in Great Britain.

74
A detailed reconstruction of a Belle
Époque station in the Chateau de La Ferte-
Saint Aubin private museum in the Loire.

74-75
The interior of a rebuilt period station
in the Chateau de La Ferte-Saint Aubin
private museum in the Loire.

In France, it is possible to travel on one
of the last meter gauge railway lines, in the
Loire, the Chemin de Fer du Blanc Argent,
which running between the towns of Lucay
Le Male and Argy is preserved and managed
as a "heritage railway" by "SABA" Societé
d'animation du Blanc Argent.

In Italy there are numerous tourist and historical train journeys made every month, but not many are actually organized to provide a regular or periodic tourist service. Among these mention must undoubtedly be made of the tourist services in spring and autumn with historic trains on the preserved lines of Palazzolo - Paratico Sarnico on Lake Iseo and Asciano - Monte Antico in Tuscany. Periodically, the trains on these lines are also pulled by steam locomotives. In Sardinia there is the "Trenino Verde" on the Mandi - Arbatax, Isili - Sorgono, Macomer - Bosa and Nulvi - Palau routes. In addition to the period diesel

railcars it is also possible to organize the trip with a steam locomotive and historic carriages. A little gem, a real fairy-tale train, is undoubtedly the Ritten Railway which crosses the plateau of the same name near Bolzano. It is a short electric tramway in regular service that passes through an enchanting landscape connecting Soprabolzano to Collalbo. From time to time the original period electric locomotive with wooden slats from the early 1900s is used;

and the round-trip ticket costs just €6. With a little patience therefore it is possible to find in Europe, but also in the rest of the world, beautiful train routes that allow travelers to savor the charm of travel on a human scale.

76
A period electric locomotive of the Ritten Railway, near Bolzano.

76-77
One of the most beautiful Italian tourist trains, the Trenino Verde in Sardinia.

INDEX

PHOTO CREDITS

AUTHOR

FRANCO TANEL, journalist and photographer began his professional career in 1979 with the photographic agency D-Day of which he was one of the founders. He has worked with the principal Italian photo-journalistic agencies, including Contrasto and Grazia Neri. He deals in particular with transport and infrastructure, sustainable tourism and, in the social field, he has been documenting the phenomenon of immigration in Italy for years. Alongside his activity as photographer he has always worked as a journalist. He contributes on the themes of transport and urban planning to *Il Sole 24 Ore* and *Tuttotreno*, the leading Italian periodical dedicated to railways. He participates as an expert in the sector at conferences and seminars on transport.

WS White Star Publishers® is a registered trademark
property of De Agostini Libri S.p.A.

© 2013 De Agostini Libri S.p.A.
Via G. da Verrazano, 15
28100 Novara, Italy
www.whitestar.it - www.deagostini.it

Translation: Contextus s.r.l., Pavia (Martin Maguire)
Editing: Contextus s.r.l., Pavia

ISBN 978-88-544-0800-5
1 2 3 4 5 6   17 16 15 14 13

Printed in China